Daily, This Book will Powerfully Change Your Mindset

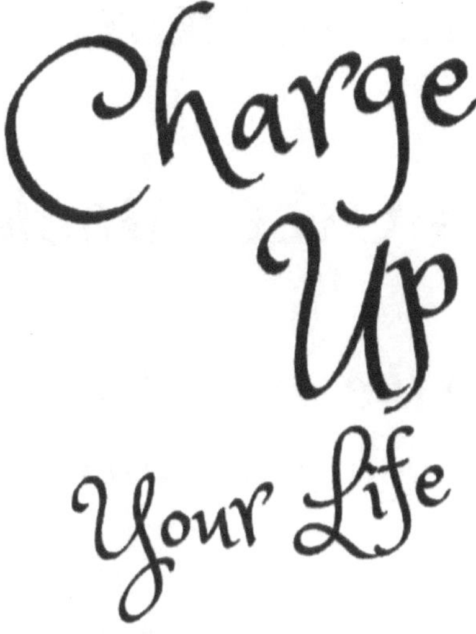


# 12 MINUTES A DAY TO SUCCESS

## CORKIE MANN

BEST SELLING AUTHOR

**Dedicated to You and Your Success**

**Corkie's Other Books:**

*"Mastering the Art of Success"*
*"Roommates to Romance"*

**Contact for Mentoring and Speaking events**

**Corkiemann.com**
**Corkie@Corkiemann.com**

# Today, Take Charge of Your Life.

I'm Going to Show
you Something,
that Once You
Understand it….
From that Moment On
**Your Life
Will Never
Be the Same**

# Today You are Committed to Being Extraordinary

The very fact that you
are reading this
Is an indication that you
are committed to a
mighty
change in your life.

# Begin Right Where You are

# Today Enjoy Your life
## Right Where You Are.

Be Happy
Right
where
you are
Right
Now.

# Your Intentions are Always Being Created in Your Life.

Whether you like what you've created or not. Whether you believe it, understand it, or not…

# It's True

# Celebrate

Your Life!
Your Good Times
And
Not So Good Times.

**Celebrate
All of Your Life!
And you will
Experience
Magic!**

You Will
Always
Attract to You
What's in
Harmony
With Your
Thoughts
and Feelings.
No Matter if they
are
Positive or Negative
thoughts & feelings

# The
# Truth
# Is...

# Whatever You Want

Dream it with
experiencing all
the feelings
Of actually
having it.

**Amazingly you
can have it.**

# Your Brain has a Reticular Activating System…RAS

Your RAS will respond to an image in your head as if it were reality.
Back in May 1957, Scientific American published an article describing the discovery of the "reticular formation" at the base of the brain ... this is basically the gateway to your conscious awareness.
When you think a thought, let's say you want a convertible car.
Thinking about it occurs in your RAS.
This part of your brain doesn't know the difference between Real and Unreal.
See it with a passionate feeling, knowing you're there. (Pretend) feel the fresh air, hear the sounds, smile, see yourself really riding in it.
Believe…and Do this every day and somehow the means for it will show up.

And it's just the same when you focus on
Not enough money, not enough love, health, fun, and feel all those "lack of" feelings… And on top of that, you'll have a "pity party" and invite your friends in on you sorrows. You are creating more and more sorrows for next week, because that's what you are focused on and more sorrow shows up even faster, because your "lack of" feelings are so strong, you might even cry… with more passion, I know I've been there.

# "A Man Is What He Thinks About All Day Long"

**Ralph Waldo Emerson**

# What do
# You
# think
# About all
# Day
# Long?

# It's all up to You

# Do
# You
# Worry?

# If Worry creep's in, Then Where is Your Faith?

# ...BELIEVE

# It's Just 3 Easy Steps
1. Ask
2. Believe
3. Receive

**From My Favorite Book:**

And all things whatsoever ye shall **ASK** in prayer **BELIEVING** ye shall **RECEIVE**.

Matthew 21:22

Therefore, I say unto you, What things soever ye Desire, when ye **PRAY, BELIEVE**, that ye **RECEIVE** them, and ye shall have them.

Mark 11:24

**ASK**, and it shall be **GIVEN** you; seek, and ye shall find; knock, and it shall be **opened** unto you.

Matthew 7:7

# You Can
# Have
# What You
# Want...
# As long as
# You
# Believe You
# Can.

# Realize that It's not possible to Worry and Believe at the same time.

# Whatever you Ask for, and Truly Believe, You can Receive it.

# You Are Creating Your Life. Right Now, Through your Thoughts, Feelings and Words.

# What You Focus On Today, Is What You Are Creating For Your Tomorrows.

# Focus
## on Negative &
## You Will
## Receive
## Negative,
## Focus on Positive
## & You Will
## Receive
## POSITIVE.
## It's All
## up to You!

# Now, add Passion, excitement, smile, laugh, act as if it's happening right now!

What you think
About, you will
Bring about.
What You say,
You will Create.
How you Feel
brings more
energy to your
thoughts.

When you are
upset about
something or
you're worrying
about it, you are
bringing more
Energy to those
Troublesome
Feelings.  This
will create more
and more to be
upset or
worry about.

Have you
ever said…
"See, I knew it
would turn out
like this."
You just knew
something bad
was going to
happen!
**Your thought
Focus Created it**

**You see!
You are Very
Powerful**
You can
**Think negative
or positive**
thoughts about
something and
**Voila!
There it is!**

# Your
# Thoughts
# are Requests
# They are a
# Silent
# Prayer.

# "If It's to Be… It's Up to Me"

William H. Johnsen

# What Do You Want? What Do You Really Truly Want?

Many people don't know
the answer to this
question.
You might need
to ask yourself…
**If I could have
anything I want
and I knew I
wouldn't fail,
what would it be?**

**The answer to
this question
Is in your
"Heart".**
It's not in your
mind.
You can't "think"
the answer to this.

# What Makes Makes You Happy?

## Really Happy!

This is where you begin to start Dreaming.

# If you had a
# few Million
# Dollars &
# Nothing
# Stopping you,
# what would
# You
# Have or Do?

# "How can
# I do it ?"
# You ask...

**To Dream is Not to be concerned about "How" to accomplish the goal.**

How will I have the money ?

**How** can I know what I need to know?

**How** will I get help or support?

**"How" is none of your business"**

# "The How" just gets in your way.

Have **Belief**, let go, and Just Intend to have what you want.

# Caution,
# Be Careful
# Know what
# you are
# asking
# for !

# Be
# Specific
# in
# Your
# Requests.

Many years ago
I prayed to meet
"Mr. Right".
I met a guy
and his last name
was Wright, and when
I realized he wasn't
"The One", I told him,
He started stalking me.
I learned a very
valuable Lesson …
God has
a sense of humor.
**Be Specific**

I realize
some
things are
just not
possible

A 65-Year-Old Woman has a
strong Desire to Become the
Quarterback for the SF 49ers.
In All Probability, This isn't
Going to happen. However,
She can Still Have the
**Same Emotions and
Feelings of rewards**
That success in football
could Create.
She Asks Herself
"What Would This Dream
Give Me?" …Fame,
Fortune, Accomplishment!
She Found, by becoming
a famous Artist instead, she
could create those
Same rewarding Feelings.

# A spark of Belief is all you need… Just a Spark

# What are You Passionate About?

"What would You dare to Dream, if You knew you wouldn't fail".

Brian Trac

**When tears
come
to your eyes,
and
your heart beats
so fast, that
your
stomach does
flips.
THAT'S IT!**

# Hold onto this Passionate Feeling!

If you Listen to the
Negative
voices, the
"yeah buts"
This will only slow you
down…
**Just hold onto your
Dream**

If it FEELS
like
it's **Forced,**
or
it's someone
else's dream
**It's not for
you.**

It's a
Magical
Feeling!
You feel so
Excited you
just
Might
Explode!

When I was a little girl, I heard a song every Sunday night on Disney that inspired me…
"You got to have a dream ...
If you don't have a dream ...
How you gonna have
your dreams come true?

Jiminy Cricket

**What is your Dream?**
You'll find it within you,
it has always been there.
You may have buried it
long ago, or it may have
even improved, but it's
there. Let go of why you
"think" you Can't have it.
**Just pretend for a
moment**
**there's nothing stopping
you. The Opportunity is
here right now!
What is it?
Hold on to it.**

# NOW
# BREATHE
# LIFE
# INTO IT !

I was 10 when I found an **Inspirational Poem "Don't Quit"** I think of it Often, and it helps to get through those tough days.

## DON'T QUIT

When things go wrong, as they sometimes will,
When the road you're trudging seems all uphill,
When the funds are low and the debts are high,
And you want to smile, but you have to sigh,
When care is pressing you down a bit-
Rest if you must, but don't you quit.
Life is queer with its twists and turns,
As every one of us sometimes learns,
And many a fellow turns about
When he might have won had he stuck it out.
So, don't give up though the pace seems slow -
You may succeed with another blow.
Often the goal is nearer than
It seems to a faint and faltering man;
Often the struggler has given up
When he might have captured the victor's cup;
And he learned too late when the night came
down,
How close he was to the golden crown.
Success is failure turned inside out -
The silver tint in the clouds of doubt,
And you never can tell how close you are,
It might be near when it seems afar;
So, stick to the fight when you're hardest hit -
It's when things seem worst that you must not
quit.
**By Anonymous**

How do we
receive
our Dreams?

**Ask**

**Believe**

**Receive**

# ASK...
# Begin Each Day By Stating Your Intention!

Today Set Your
Intention.
**Know it's Yours!
Have Complete
Faith,
Nothing
Wavering.**
This is not just a
Wish or a Hope,
**It is your
INTENTION.
Feel the difference in
Your
Intentional Power!**

In the movie…
"Grumpier Old
Men" Pop said,
"Well, you can
WISH in one
hand
and crap in the
other and see
which gets filled
first."

# Wishing, Always Keeps Your Desires in the future.

KNOW like you KNOW, like you KNOW… That it's REAL.

Lisa Nichols

# Know That it Really is… For REAL.

You see, we all have the asking part down perfectly. We hope, and we wish, and we want, but that's always in the future. It's always someday…in a far away time, in a far away place…that you don't really expect to happen.

# Believe

It's the Believing part
that we have a bit of
trouble with.
Why else would you
worry about it?
**If you know it's in
"the Works" and it
IS on its way to
you…
Then why would you
need to worry?**

Set Your
Intention
**And Your
Dream
Is
90%
Complete.**

There will be
Opportunities
that
will just show up
"out of the blue".
They may seem a
bit weird, odd or
different.
All you need
to do is
Act on them.

**Your Job is to get out of the Way.**

When you Worry, or
have Doubts and
Fears about
"How" it's going to
happen,
That's When
You get in Your own
way.
Be happy and relax…
get out of your own
way.

# "Don't Worry Be Happy"

**Bobby McFerrin**

This is my message in a nutshell.
Just Follow Bobby's advice,
And You will have it All!

Stuff will show up, that will make it look like it's not ever going to happen... That's a Test of Your Conviction. Don't Give Up!

# Relax,
## & Trust...
## Your
## Dream
## is on its way
## to you right
## now.

# Hold onto
# your
# Intention

# Now,
# get Excited
# about It!
# Feel All the
# Joyful
# feelings
# you'll have
# Obtaining it!

**That's Passion!
Passion is the
Rocket
Fuel for your
Desires!**
No Matter What
Comes your way
to stop you, keep
your focus, desire,
and determination.

# Be grateful for the good and the bad!!!! Your goal will arrive much faster when you Are grateful for it all!

It's usually right at your doorstep at the moment you feel like quitting.

Gratitude is
Powerful
Be Grateful for
Everything!
Give Thanks
for all you have,
no matter what
it looks like
right now.

# Take Calculated Risks

The person who
takes no chances
generally
has to take whatever
is left over, when
everyone else is
done choosing.

# Listen To Your Intuition

Your intuition is not your mind… it's your heart & your feelings.

# Now, Apply Massive Action to your Intuition, and to the Opportunities that come your way.

**When You are Happy, Trusting your Intuition, Loving your Life, You're on the right path to your dream.**

The Opportunities
That could bring
you to Your
Dreams,
Are Always
Coming to You.
But, if you are
having a
"Pity Party",
the Opportunity
will pass you by.

Opportunities are just like Radio Waves. If you're on channel 8, which might be Worry.  Happiness Comes in on Channel 2, Then the Happiness waves are passing you by. You're just not on the right channel to receive them.

It's up to you to
Feel Joyful,
Happy,
Satisfied,
and Grateful.
By doing this,
you
will change the
channel.

# Today, Choose Your Emotion !

I Love to Paint!
And It Brings
Such Joy to Me.
And Now That I am
In a State of Joy…
The Opportunities for
My Intention, Which
Have Nothing to Do
with Painting,
Are Free
Flowing, and Come
Much Faster.

Try it…
Do what
makes you
Feel Happy!
Play!
Lighten up!

**Only You
Can Make YOU
Feel Good
About
Yourself**
And
There is only one
person that can
make you feel bad
about yourself
YOU

# Be Full Of Happiness.

Complaining Only Creates your Tomorrow to have More to Complain About.

# Complaining Is Repulsive!
It
Repels all Happiness.

# Focus On Your Dreams With Excitement

# Thought Patterns

Scientists have proven that when we have the same thoughts over and over throughout our lives (autopilot), we actually make grooves in our brain. Thoughts like…You'll never amount to anything, you can't do that, we don't have enough money/time. These become autopilot thoughts, And they create your life. Scientists have also discovered that when you Stop the Autopilot thoughts and think new thoughts, the old grooves dissolve and the new thoughts create New Grooves in your brain. FOR REAL ! So, to Change your life, Change your thoughts! Change the grooves in your brain. Now, you can have new autopilot beliefs! I'm smart, I'm successful, I'm attractive, I'm loving.

Once You
Make Up
Your Mind
As to
What You
Want, All the
Obstacles
Seem
to Vanish.

# Make up Your Mind as to what Your Intention is. Make a Decision Right Now, and Go for It!

# Focus Only on the "End Result"

As Forest Gump Did. He Didn't Worry About the Fact that at first, he only caught 5 shrimp.
He Just Knew He Was a Successful "Shrimpin Boat Captain."

**Say to Yourself:
"I Don't know
How,
and I Don't
Need to
Know How...
...I Just Know
my dreams are
Real"
Stay focused on
the End Result**

# Keep Doing What You're Doing.

Keep Your Job, Keep Everything "AS IS" and Focus on Your INTENTION

"Our Doubts
Are Traitors
And Make Us
Lose The
Good
We Oft Might
Win, By
Fearing
To Attempt."
**William Shakespeare**

"**Think You Can Or Think You Can't Either Way You Are Right**"

Henry Ford

# The Impossible Ford V-8 Motor.

Henry Ford's engineers all agreed that it was impossible to create a V-8 Motor. Ford said "Produce it anyway". After many months of trying every conceivable plan, the engineers all agreed it was Impossible.

Ford Said "Go right ahead", "I want it and I'll have it." The engineers went ahead, and after 2 years, it is said that **"By a Stroke of good luck" they developed the V-8 Motor.**

Now that you are
focusing with
happiness
and intention for
your dreams, new
thoughts and
opportunities are
coming your way.
Be Aware of them,
and If it feels right,
go after them, this is
how Your Dreams
become reality.

Once you start
Believing,
you'll
start Creating.
**Watch for all
opportunities**
that come your
way.

"No Man Can Get Rich Himself, Unless He Enriches Others."

"Your Returns in Life are in Direct Proportion to What You GIVE."

**Earl Nightingale**

# Give...
# Without
# Expectation

# Integrity

is Essential.
Only Make
Promises You
Will Keep.  Be
Honest with
Everyone,
Especially with
Yourself.
**Do What You
Say You'll Do!**

**When You Feel
the
Intuitive Nudge
Say YES!
As long As It's
Legal, Moral,
Ethical, and
Your
Inner Voice Says
"Okay"...DO IT!**

If you say
"I'll Try"
Realize that
**"Trying" is just**
**Another**
**Word For**
**"I'm Not Doing**
**It!"**
Try To Stand
Up???

"Try
Not....
Do,
or Do Not...
There is No
TRY"
Jedi Master Yoda

# True Wealth
## Is a combination
## of all…

Freedom, Family
Respect, Love
Relationships
Joy, Finance
Peace, Spirituality
Harmony
Gratitude
Happiness &
Health

# Believe

### and then

# Relax,

## Your Intention
## is Happening
## Right Now!

Stuff is going to
happen that you
won't like, it may
even upset you, or
make you Angry. It
may have you
believing your
Dream won't ever
Happen.

# Trust

# It's

# on its

# way.

We all view our
lives
differently.
We all have
choices.
Have you ever
seen a rich
man sad, or a
poor man
joyful?

It's all just a choice. Decide to be joyful. Find something that makes you happy. Shift your Paradigm

# To Change Your Paradigm

Is to Change
The Way You
View Things…
Look at
Youtube.com
Nick Vujicic

"If You Want to Take Small Incremental Steps, Change Your Behavior.
If You Want to Take Quantum Leaps, Change Your Paradigm"
Stephen Covey

What if your Results don't fit your pictures?
Let it Be okay, and be Grateful.
It may seem to start out Different.
Play the "Perfect game" Your results could be even better.

# Just Relax, and stay Focused The "How" Will Show Up.

# Be Careful, because your Mind May Steer You Astray.

Your mind only wants you to stay just the way you are, in your soft cozy little comfort zone.

**Your Comfort Zone is exactly that… Comfortable. Non-Exploring, non-adventurist, and not allowing you to live your Dreams. It may be comfortable but look at all that you are sacrificing.**

**Your Mind can keep your Emotional Vibrations Down.**
Who Else Tells You
"You're Fat?" or "That Was a
Dumb thing to do!"
Who Tells You, You Can't do
something, you're too Old or Too
Young, to big or too small, or you
don't have enough time, or money
to do it. Your mind gives you all
the reasons why you can't do
something.
Who Keeps you up at night and
won't let you Sleep?
And you tell it
to "Shut Up" and it says
"I can't, I have all these things
to worry about!"
Matthew Ferry

**Most of the Time
Your MIND will
attempt to**
Steer you off course,
and **Keep you from
Succeeding, because
of all the belief
patterns that
you have had for
all your life.**
You'll Know when
You should listen to
your mind. Think about
giving a good
friend the same advice.

# Listen to Your Heart! Your Mind can steer you off course.

**Procrastination Will keep you from Living Your Dreams.** Your mind encourages you to procrastinate and keep you safe in your comfort zone.

# Everyday apply Massive Action to what your HEART Speaks to You. Listen to your Intuition

## How can you tell if it's your Intuition?
Anything New and
Different
Comes from Inner
Voice, Your Intuition.
If your heart beats faster,
you have butterflies in
your stomach, you get all
choked up. You might
feel tingly all over, and
get a great big smile on
your face, or maybe even
get teary eyed…
That's it!

**Your Mind is
speaking**
when you hear
anything
that comes from
**lessons from your
past, warnings,
worries, or
concerns.**
Nagging voices from
your childhood, are
all from your Mind
and should be taken
with a "grain of salt".

Of Course,
There are things we
need to listen to… there
are real dangers
to avoid.
**Ask yourself, "Am I in
real
danger here, what is
the worst thing
that could happen?"**
"If I get too close to the
edge could I fall off of
the cliff?" "If I make
that scary phone call
will I survive?"

# Is your life on Auto Pilot?

Have you ever been driving somewhere, and when you arrived you couldn't remember the trip?

Be aware and awake to feel those quiet little Nudges.

**When new Opportunities come by, be aware of them. Look into them.** It may not appear to be the answer, but this is how your **Dreams come to** reality… **Through other people.**

# Today's a Brand New Day, clean with no mistakes!

*Anne of Green Gables*

Let Go of Yesterday!
Know Your Intention!
Let Go and Be Happy!

## FEEL GOOD!

Even if you feel just a little bit better than yesterday.

There was a time when I didn't have cable TV for a few months, and I could only watch movies of my choice. When I had the Cable turned on again, I found myself more negative.
I figured it out!
**The Negative News**!
The news, is no longer "on" in my house. I've been so creative, happy and "in charge" of my life ever since.
I always somehow seem to find out the important stuff I need to know.

Watch funny
movies, or Turn
off the TV
Get off the
Couch And
**Do something
Fun
that makes you
Happy.**

"People are Always Blaming Their Circumstances for The Way They Are. The People Who Get On In This World Are the People Who Get Up and Look for the Circumstances They Want, And If They Can't Find Them, MAKE THEM!"

George B. Shaw

# Do What Makes You Happy.

Play your favorite
Music, Sing, Dance,
Play, Dream.
Find a place
you love to be
and go there,
even if it's in your
own mind.

# Suffering
# Is a Choice
All Suffering is
Repulsive…
It Repels All That
You Want.
**All Suffering of
Guilt, Fear, Hate,
Sadness, Worry, etc.
Repels Your
Dreams.**
Stop it!

**Holding onto
grudges will
cause you to Suffer.
FORGIVENESS
Is necessary for you to
BE FREE.**
Forgive Those Who Have
Wronged You, No Matter
How Severe.
See Good Happening
In Their Lives.
**Forgiveness Is the
Greatest Gift You Can
Give Yourself.**

Hatred, Anger, and
Stubbornness, Will
Only Poison
Your Life.
**Love Those Who
Have Wronged
You,
Think positive
thoughts of them,
And You Will
Become Free
Once Again.**

Love yourself
enough to Take
the pain and
hurt out of
your life…
Forgive!
Just try it…
Forgive others,
and Especially
forgive
Yourself.

# Money Matters:

Realize that "Being broke is a temporary situation. Being poor is a state of mind." Whatever you say is what you are creating.

Hold onto
one
Thought at a
time…
and Watch It
Grow.

When You Focus
on too Many
Things, it's Like
Trying to
**Start a Fire with
a Magnifying
Glass, While
Moving It
Around.**
It Never Stays
Still Long Enough
to Catch on Fire.

# Read Biography's,

Like Walt Disney,
Bob Hope,
Henry Ford,
Lee Iacocca, and
more.

**They knew what they wanted, and there was no doubt they were going to have it.**

# "All your dreams can come true, if you have the Courage to pursue them"
**Walt Disney**

# Today you've Realized your Desires!

**Feel good about them
Right now!
Yes, before they arrive.**
"The Package of your
desires is in the mail on its
way to you right now",
be grateful!
You've planted the seed,
it's on its way, pushing its
way right up through the
moist warm dirt". Use **your
imagination everyday**

# You Have the
# Power to
# Choose Your
# Life
# Right Now.
# Get Ready
# and
# Go for it!

Use your
Imagination
skills and
Act "As If" The
Thing You
Desire…
Your Intention…
Is Real, and in
Your
Possession
Right Now.

Come on, close
your eyes and
see it, feel it,
smell it, and get
excited about it!
**Celebrate
Receiving it!
Then Let Go,
Really, Let Go
and receive it!**

"Thank
God For
Unanswered
Prayers"
Garth Brooks

"I could have
missed
the Pain, But I'd
have had to
miss …
The Dance"
Garth Brooks

# Remember
# It's
# Already
# Yours!
# Enjoy the
# Ride

# Now,
# Apply
# Massive
# Action.
# Go for it!

# "Quitters Never Win and Winners Never Quit"

**Napoleon Hill**

"I worked For a Menial's Hire, Only to Learn Dismayed, That Any Wage I had Asked of Life, Life Would Have Willingly Paid."
Napoleon Hill

**"When Riches begin to Come, They Come So Quickly, and in Such Great Abundance, That One Wonders Where They Have Been Hiding During All Those Lean Years."**

**Napoleon Hill**

**Have a Heart
Filled with
Gratitude All
Day long.
You May Not Have
the Things You
Want Right Now.
Focus on
What You
DO Have,
and Appreciate it
daily.**

# Being Grateful
# Today
# Will Create
# More
# To Be Grateful
# For
# Tomorrow!
# BE HAPPY
# NOW!

Be Grateful
for that home
that's too
small, or your
car that
needs fixed, or
the job you
don't like.

**Be Grateful
for the lessons
you've
Learned in
Life…
They have taken
You to where
You are right
Now**

"Human
Beings Can
Alter Their
Lives by
Altering
Their
Attitudes."
William James

"All I've Got
is
Persistence…
Turns Out
That's All
You Need"
Darren LaCroix

# RELAX! Your Intention is Now Set

Stay
focused
on the
End Result,
Have Faith,
and the
Rest will
Follow!

**For the Next
90 Days
Read the bold
words in this
book
10 minutes a Day
Internalize it.
Believing,
Knowing,
With
Unwavering
Faith**

# All The Power you Ever need is always there, whether you use it or not, is Your Choice!

# You are Powerful ! You Can Live Your Dreams !

* 9 7 9 8 6 5 3 9 4 7 5 7 5 *